This Book Belongs To:

Color Test Page

fuck off
I'm coloring

Value yourself
and others

SOMETIMES
LIFE SUCK

Positive thinking
makes it happen

Adopt the pace of nature: her secret is patience.

- Ralph Waldo Emerson

Love yourself
and others

Things i want to
say at work
but can't

JUST Breathe

The best bridge
between despair and hope
is a good night's sleep.
E. Joseph Cossman

live
laugh
love

WHEN THE
flower blooms,
the bees
COME UNINVITED.

- Ramakrishna

Never
fucking
give up

Every day is
a good
day

I can't
fix stupid

Create your own Reality

Life
IS
LIKE
A
ROAD
trip
Enjoy each day
BUT
don't carry
too much
BAGGAGE

As the sun shines both on the cedar tree and the smallest flower, so the Divine sun illumines each soul.
Therese of Lisieux

INHALE THE GOOD SHIT EXHALE THE BULLSHIT

Open your
heart to your dreams

Be the
BEST
fuck the
rest

Life
IS LIKE A
Cup of Tea
IT'S ALL IN HOW YOU
make it

cheer the fuck up

calm the
fuck down

Harmony
brings health
and happiness

Life IS LIKE A THORNY but Beautiful

www.ingramcontent.com/pod-product-compliance
Lightning Source LLC
LaVergne TN
LVHW081805050326
832903LV00027B/2108
9798692671332